W9-AAT-828

ADHD

Trudi Strain Trueit

Franklin Watts
A Division of Scholastic Inc.
New York • Toronto • London • Auckland • Sydney
Mexico City • New Delhi • Hong Kong
Danbury, Connecticut

Dedication

For those with ADHD and the people who love them

Cover design by Robert O'Brien.
Interior design by Kathleen Santini.
Illustration p. 36 by Pat Rasch.

Library of Congress Cataloging-in-Publication Data

Trueit, Trudi Strain.
    ADHD / by Trudi Strain Trueit.
        v. cm. — (Life balance)
Contents: In fast forward—Exploring ADHD—Pieces of the puzzle—Brainworks—Pinpointing ADHD.
    ISBN 0-531-12261-1 (lib. bdg.)   0-531-15580-3 (pbk.)
1. Attention-deficit hyperactivity disorder—Juvenile literature.
    [1. Attention-deficit hyperactivity disorder.] I. Title. II. Series.
    RJ506.H9T78 2004
    618.92′8589—dc21

                                2003007154

Table of Contents

One

In Fast Forward

Daniel was in trouble again. After waving his hand in the air for what seemed like forever, Daniel called out to his teacher for help. Ms. Donnelly asked him to wait and said she would be with him when she finished helping another student. Daniel tried hard to be patient, but it wasn't easy. He tapped his pencil against the edge of the desk. He tore the corner off his paper, crumpled it into a ball, and flicked it around the desk. He even tried humming to himself. Yet, a minute or so later, Daniel was out of his seat, asking other students if they knew what to do.

Soon, he was stuck in the "chill chair," the seat right next to Ms. Donnelly's desk that was reserved for students who could not behave. "Sit here, be quiet, and finish your work, Daniel," said his teacher firmly. With everyone in class staring at him, Daniel felt embarrassed. This was the third time in two weeks he'd had to sit in the chill chair. His parents were going to hear about this for sure, and boy, were they going to be angry.

Daniel's mom and dad describe him as a kid "in fast forward." He's been that way for as long as they can remember. Highly excitable, Daniel doesn't have what his father calls "stick-to-it-iveness," unless he's doing an activity that he loves, such as playing video games. Daniel doesn't seem to want to take responsibility for anything. He rarely wakes up on time for school. On most days, his mom has to drag him out of bed. He doesn't help out much around the house. If his parents ask him to do something, he might mumble "yes" and start the job, but he never finishes it. He has constant squabbles with his brother and sister over little things, such as what to watch on television. He has much bigger arguments with his parents regarding his messy room and his "lazy attitude."

Over the years, life at school hasn't gotten any smoother. Daniel's second-grade teacher compared his behavior to that of a bumblebee that flits from flower to flower, but never settles on one for very long. Now in the sixth grade, Daniel races through assignments quickly and makes careless mistakes. Many times, he gets distracted and forgets to finish his homework altogether. His handwriting and spelling are so bad that those papers he does complete are often turned back to him to do over. Although he's doing well in math and enjoys it, Daniel has fallen behind in reading. It is hard for him to focus on a book. He loses interest and his mind wanders. "This shouldn't be happening. You're a bright student," Ms. Donnelly has said to him more than once. "If you'd slow down and apply yourself, you would do so much better." Her words of disappointment only echo what he has heard from many teachers many times before.

Daniel wants to please his teacher and parents, but he is bubbling with so much energy that he often feels like a rocket about to blast off. He can't stop drumming his fingers on the desk and kicking the legs of Tim's chair in front of him. (Tim is getting pretty annoyed about it, too.) Daniel wishes that the two of them could be friends. He doesn't have a good friend. When Daniel moved to town a year ago, he quickly fit in. At first, kids liked the way he'd clowned around. Yet, one by one, each of his new friends had drifted away. He knew why. In sports, Daniel insisted on being the leader, telling everyone what to play and how to play it. If he was losing or someone on his team made a mistake, Daniel became upset, even though he knew he shouldn't. He'd kick the dirt. He'd yell. Many times, he'd stomp off in a huff. Twice, he's gotten into a fistfight.

Can You Relate?

- Do you usually have a hard time sitting still at your desk?
- Do you constantly interrupt people or intrude on others when they are talking?
- Do people tell you that you talk too much, or do you get in trouble a lot for talking?
- Do you often get too "hyper" and find it hard to calm down?
- Do other kids frequently avoid you or tell you they don't want to be around you?
- Do you tend to race through things, such as school-work or eating dinner?
- Are you apt to daydream when you are supposed to be listening to the teacher?
- Is it hard for you to concentrate on tasks, especially those that are not very interesting to you?

- Is your desk, locker, or bedroom really messy?
- Do you find that school or homework is usually boring?
- Does it seem like you have been struggling in school since day one?
- Do you often forget things?
- Does it feel like you're always getting in trouble at home and at school?

If you answered "yes" to more than a few of the above questions, you might have ADHD. However, there could be other things going on that are causing these difficulties, such as stress, anxiety, depression, hearing or vision problems, or a learning disability. If you are having problems, don't ignore them. Talk to your parents about your concerns, and don't be afraid to seek help from a doctor or mental health professional.

Now, nobody plays with him. He spends breaks bouncing a ball alone on the basketball court. That is how Daniel feels most of the time—alone. He doesn't intend to drive his friends away, get into trouble, or make his parents angry, yet that is exactly what he always seems to be doing. "What," he wonders, "is wrong with me?"

In the Shadow of ADHD

Everyone can relate to some of Daniel's experiences. You might accidentally blurt out a question in class or hurry through an assignment without checking your work. Kids have tons of energy, so it's natural for you to want to stretch and move after sitting in a quiet classroom all morning. At sporting events, who hasn't gotten angry after losing a hard-fought game? Yet, while these things happen to most of us just once in a while, they happen to Daniel far more frequently and more intensely than what is considered normal for a kid his age. His behavior problems are creating difficulties at home, hurting his grades, and costing him friendships. Daniel's teacher suspects he may have attention-deficit/hyperactivity disorder, or ADHD for short. She will recommend to his parents that they see the school counselor and his pediatrician to find out more about Daniel's behavior.

ADHD is the most common behavioral disorder found in American children. A behavioral disorder is a continual pattern of abnormal behavior that is determined by many factors, such as a person's words, actions, and how he or she responds to certain situations. It causes serious and ongoing problems in someone's daily life. A child is considered to have a behavioral disorder when his or her everyday behavior severely interferes with social and academic progress.

Most scientists agree that ADHD has a biological cause that involves slight differences in the brain. You cannot "catch" ADHD the way you would a cold or flu. It's either a natural part of who you are, or it isn't. This doesn't mean that someone with ADHD isn't responsible for what he or she says and does. It does mean that it may be more of a challenge for that person than for most people to control his or her behavior.

The American Psychiatric Association (APA) estimates that one to three million kids in the United States have ADHD. The APA defines the main symptoms of ADHD as having severe and continual problems with attention, hyperactivity (over-activity), and impulsive behavior (acting without first thinking of the consequences). There is no way to prevent or cure ADHD. However, with successful treatment, most people with the disorder can lead happy, healthy lives.

A Hot Topic

ADHD is a controversial disorder. There is debate over nearly every aspect of ADHD, from what causes it to ways to treat it.

Although doctors know a great deal about the disorder, they still have much to learn. This is one reason many people are at odds about it. Researchers estimate that every classroom in the United States typically has one or two kids with ADHD. Yet some health professionals say it is being diagnosed too often, especially in younger kids. They fear ADHD is being used as an excuse to medicate children who have not learned or been taught proper self-discipline. Others argue that ADHD is not a medical condition at all, but rather a personality type. With this much apparent disagreement going on, you may wonder if ADHD is real.

There is debate over nearly every aspect of ADHD, from what causes it to ways to treat it.

In the year 2000, the National Institutes of Health (NIH), a government health organization, concluded that the scientific evidence presented throughout the past century clearly proves that ADHD does exist. Similarly, the American Medical Association, the American Academy of Pediatrics, the U.S. Surgeon General, and the U.S. Department of Education all recognize ADHD as a real disorder. In January 2002, nearly ninety scientists from around the world teamed up to publish a statement on ADHD. They wanted to set the record straight that the majority of the international scientific community regards ADHD as a true medical condition.

The Name Game

Over the past fifty years, ADHD has gone through many name changes. It used to be called attention deficit disorder (ADD) when symptoms dealt with inattention only. Later, it was changed to attention deficit disorder with hyperactivity (ADD-H) when symptoms of inattention as well as hyperactivity and impulsivity were present. In 1994, the American Psychiatric Association grouped the two into one category, attention-deficit/hyperactivity disorder. (Not everyone who has the disorder has symptoms of overactivity, so a slash is used to signify that hyperactivity may or may not be present.) Health professionals continue to debate whether ADHD is the most accurate description for the disorder, so it's likely there will be more name changes in the future.

The scientists were also concerned that inaccurate stories being reported in the media could be causing thousands of people with ADHD to avoid seeking help.

In this book, you'll read about the issues at the heart of the ADHD debate. You'll learn the symptoms, possible causes, and methods of treatment. You'll also read firsthand accounts from kids whose lives were touched—and changed—by what can be a devastating disorder.

Two

Exploring ADHD

Have you ever started cleaning your room, but then got distracted and didn't finish the job? Did you ever lose anything important, such as lunch money or your house key? Have you ever been so anxious you couldn't stop bouncing in the car and calling out, "Are we there yet?" Most of us can answer "yes" to these questions. At certain times, you've let your chores slide, misplaced an item, or found yourself unable to contain your excitement. Even though you occasionally do these things, it does not mean you have ADHD.

So how can you tell if you or someone you know has ADHD? It is not an easy question to answer, because ADHD is not an easy disorder to diagnose. There is no blood test or mental exam that someone can take to prove he or she has ADHD. A diagnosis is subjective, meaning it depends on the opinions of the health professionals collecting the information. Some people have expressed concern over this. They say if doctors cannot test for ADHD, how can they tell if someone has it? ADHD experts argue that there is no lab test for the common cold, either, but doctors can certainly tell by the symptoms—sore throat, runny nose, cough—when someone has a cold. Similarly, they say ADHD also has a very specific set of symptoms.

In 1994, the American Psychiatric Association (APA) established guidelines for diagnosing the disorder (see chart on page 21). According to the APA, in order for a diagnosis of ADHD to be considered, serious problems with attention, hyperactivity, and impulsive behavior must first appear before the age of seven and continue for at least six months. They must cause severe problems in at least two areas of life, such as at home and at school. Other settings in which ADHD can be disruptive include the school bus, band, social events, sports, clubs, and scouting.

Remember, children with ADHD experience symptoms more seriously and more often than what is typical for friends or classmates of the same age. ADHD interferes with their ability to lead a normal, joyful life. So, even if you wriggle in your seat, get in trouble for talking, or "zone out" once in a while in class, it doesn't necessarily mean you have ADHD.

Types of ADHD

ADHD affects people in very different ways. One person may have trouble with inattentiveness, but is not hyperactive or impulsive, while someone else shows signs of hyperactivity, yet is not easily distracted. Usually, though, hyperactivity and impulsiveness go hand in hand. The APA has identified three subtypes of ADHD: inattentive type, hyperactive-impulsive type, and combined type (a mix of symptoms from inattentive and hyperactive-impulsive).

Inattentive Type

Inattentive type is characterized by an inability to concentrate on a particular task or pay attention. Kids with this kind of ADHD may "tune out" other people, especially when they are bored, and may miss important directions from a teacher or parent. They may be easily distracted and move quickly from one activity to the next. Homework and other chores may not get finished. They often rush through assignments and make careless mistakes.

Because a person's attention is not always focused on the job at hand, someone with inattentive type ADHD may be labeled as "lazy," "a slacker," or "a daydreamer." That's what happened to fourteen-year-old Lily. "I would be in class taking notes and start thinking about other stuff, like how cool the leaves were on the trees outside," she recalls.

"Before I knew it, class was over and I hadn't written down more than a sentence or two. I'd have to borrow someone's notes to take home to copy. The worst part was when the teacher would call on me. I didn't know the answer because I didn't hear the question. Everybody would laugh, and I would be embarrassed because I knew they were thinking, 'What a ditz.'"

Actually, Lily is very smart. She gets A's in the subjects that hold a special interest for her and in which she gets immediate feedback from her teachers. "When I get to do things I love, like art, I can paint for hours," she says. "But if I'm bored, like I am in social studies, I shut down. All we ever do is read the book and answer the list of questions at the end of the chapter. It's a real fight to get myself through it."

Most students can manage to muddle through a boring assignment or a dull video and still remain focused, but those with inattentive ADHD are not able to do so. "I just float away like the tide," says Lily. "I try to stay in the moment, but my mind is pulled in another direction."

Sometimes, teachers and parents may miss the signs of inattentive ADHD. Because a child isn't hyperactive or impulsive, the symptoms most people associate with ADHD, the disorder may go unnoticed for several years. Lily's ADHD wasn't caught until the end of eighth grade, though she had been having problems throughout most of elementary school.

Hyperactive-Impulsive Type

Kids with hyperactive-impulsive type ADHD tend to have behavioral issues that are more readily seen and disliked by others. The word *hyper* is Greek for "above." Someone who is hyperactive gets excited over or above what is considered normal. Symptoms of hyperactivity include fidgeting, kicking, talking excessively, making noises, getting up and walking around the classroom, and bothering other students. Also, hyperactive children may find it hard to respond to requests from parents and teachers. They may have difficulty cooperating and compromising with others. This can make working in a small group very challenging. Kids with this type of ADHD may be labeled as "stubborn," "unable to be disciplined," "negative," or "rigid."

As you grow, you learn to think about the consequences

of your actions before you do things. But many kids with hyperactive-impulsive ADHD act emotionally younger than their age. They have trouble controlling their impulses, or urges. This is known as impulsivity. It may cause someone with ADHD to act or react too quickly. A person might interrupt others to make a point, say something others think is rude, or not wait his or her turn. Impulsivity may also mean doing something crazy, like trying a dangerous skateboard trick or a dare, just because it sounds fun. Some kids with hyperactive-impulsive ADHD are often said to have "a quick temper" or "a short fuse." It may not happen every day, but they can quickly lose control of their emotions when things don't go their way. They throw tantrums, get into fights, or simply pout and sulk. Many times classmates view them as "bossy," "pushy," or "aggressive." Because of this, kids with hyperactive-impulsive ADHD may find it hard to keep friends.

Combined Type

Combined type ADHD is a mixture of symptoms from both inattentive type and hyperactive-impulsive type. Between 50 and 70 percent of kids with ADHD fit into this category. "My body just can't sit still," explains Andrew, who has combined type ADHD. "I can pay attention if I'm up and moving around or I can sit still if I'm not paying attention. But I can't do both things at once."

The Signs of ADHD

To help them diagnose ADHD, health professionals rely on the following guidelines set by the American Psychiatric Association.

Six or more symptoms from one of the lists below must be present for at least six months before that particular type of ADHD is diagnosed. For combined type ADHD, a minimum of six symptoms from *each* column must occur for at least six months. (reprinted with permission from the *Diagnostic and Statistical Manual of Mental Disorders, Text revision* © 2000 American Psychiatric Association)

Inattentive Type	Hyperactive-Impulsive Type
The child often fails to give close attention to details or makes careless mistakes	The child often fidgets and squirms in his/her seat
Often has a hard time keeping his/her attention focused on tasks or play	Frequently gets up when he/she is expected to remain seated
Often easily distracted from his/her work by other things	Often has difficulty working or playing quietly
Frequently does not seem to listen when spoken to (may appear to be daydreaming)	Is continually restless or climbs/runs excessively when it is not appropriate
Does not follow through on instructions and fails to finish schoolwork, chores, and activities	Is often "on the go" or acts as if driven by a motor
Has difficulty organizing tasks and activities	Often talks excessively

The Signs of ADHD *(Continued)*	
Inattentive Type	**Hyperactive-Impulsive Type**
Often loses things, such as books, assignments, toys, and school supplies	Frequently has difficulty waiting for his/her turn
Is frequently forgetful in daily activities	Often interrupts or intrudes on others
Avoids, dislikes, or doesn't want to do tasks that require focused attention, such as homework	Frequently blurts out answers before questions are completed

All subtypes of ADHD may cause a person to struggle with planning, organization, and problem-solving skills. Someone with the disorder may develop skills more unevenly than other kids of the same age. For instance, an ADHD child may be a whiz at math, but lag behind in reading. Also, about half of all kids with the disorder have a hard time with activities that require good motor skills and coordination, such as coloring, cutting with scissors, riding a bike, or playing sports.

A Challenging Disorder

The symptoms of ADHD can vary widely from person to person. Even those with the same type of ADHD may act quite differently. Some kids may have only mild symptoms, while others may experience much more severe problems. Also, as a child grows and changes, the symptoms of ADHD may change too. Depending on the individual, some symptoms can worsen, while others get better. Frequently, kids with hyperactive-impulsive type or combined type ADHD find that as they reach their teen years, their symptoms of excessive activity decrease and are replaced by an internal restlessness. Researchers used to think that all kids outgrew ADHD by the time they became adults, but now know this is not true. Most children with ADHD carry symptoms of their disorder with them into adulthood.

Someone with ADHD is often told by others to "get organized," "quit daydreaming," "stop being a troublemaker," or "have some self-control." He or she might be viewed as deliberately behaving badly or intentionally not listening. Yet, those with ADHD do not misbehave on purpose. In fact, they can even tell you what type of behavior is appropriate in certain situations. But actually carrying out that proper behavior is the challenge. Those with ADHD don't plan to get so excited at a birthday party that they knock over the punch bowl. They don't intend to jump into other people's conversations uninvited. They don't mean to hit a friend who doesn't agree with them. Still, these things happen. Why? In the next chapter, you'll read about what scientists know—and don't know—about ADHD.

Three

Pieces of the
Puzzle

n 1902, British physician Dr. George Still was one of the first modern doctors to detect symptoms of ADHD in children, but it wasn't called ADHD then. There was no medical name for the excitable, defiant, and inattentive behavior Still witnessed. He referred to it as "volitional inhibition." At the turn of the twentieth century, troublesome behavior in children was thought to be the result of bad or neglectful parenting. But the group of misbehaving kids Still observed had been raised in what appeared to be loving, stable homes. He wondered if there were a biological reason for what was occurring. Could this unruly behavior be inherited, or passed down from one generation to the next?

Fidgety Philip

In the mid-1800s, German psychiatrist Dr. Heinrich Hoffman penned a poem that is, perhaps, the first literary reference to what we now call ADHD. Following is an excerpt of the poem:

The Story of Fidgety Philip

"Let me see if Philip can
Be a little gentleman;
Let me see if he is able
To sit still for once at the table."
Thus Papa bade Phil behave;
And Mama looked very grave.
But Fidgety Phil,
He won't sit still;
He wriggles,
And giggles,
And then, I declare,
Swings backwards and forwards,
And tilts up his chair,
Just like any rocking horse-
"Philip! I am getting cross!"
See the naughty, restless child
Growing still more rude and wild,
Till his chair falls over quite.
Philip screams with all his might,
Catches at the cloth, but then
That makes matters worse again.

Still discovered that the family histories of some of the twenty kids he studied were riddled with other behavioral and health issues, such as depression and alcoholism. Still's early studies of ADHD broke new ground on two fronts: first, it helped show that other medical problems frequently accompany ADHD, and second, that the disorder could be inherited.

A Complex Twist

Since Still's pioneering work in the field of ADHD, scientists have learned that more than half of all kids with ADHD have other psychological disorders and health issues as well. Some of the most frequent disorders that accompany ADHD are learning disabilities, oppositional defiant disorder, conduct disorder, and depression. Less common are sleep disorders, eating disorders, and anxiety.

Up to 50 percent of those with ADHD suffer from a learning disability. Connected to the way the brain processes information, a learning disability interferes with someone's ability to store or recall information. It creates a "gap" between someone's intelligence and how he or she performs, often keeping the person from achieving up to his or her actual intellectual ability. A person with a learning disability (also called a learning disorder) may struggle with memory, handwriting, understanding words and meanings, or sequencing (putting objects in the correct order). This can slow development in the areas of reading, spelling, and math.

"I have trouble reading out loud," says twelve-year-old Jonah, who has ADHD and a reading disability. "I skip words and lose my place a lot. The words get jumbled on the page." Jonah also has trouble remembering and retaining what he has just read. Even so, he is a good student and in the top 10 percent of his class. This is not surprising, because ADHD and learning disabilities have nothing to do with intelligence. Sometimes, those with ADHD and/or learning disabilities are called "underachievers" because their disorders are holding them back from what they are truly capable of doing. Today, Jonah is getting extra help at school with his learning disability so that he may reach his full potential.

ADHD and learning disabilities have nothing to do with intelligence.

Oppositional defiant disorder (ODD) is one of the most common conditions that occur alongside ADHD. About 60 percent of boys and 30 percent of girls with ADHD display signs of ODD. It is characterized by an ongoing pattern of disobedient, negative, and hostile behavior toward adults for at least six months.

If left untreated, ODD may progress to what is known as conduct disorder (CD). This is a more extreme form of defiance.

Kevin's Story: ADHD Plus ODD

"From kindergarten through the second grade, Kevin was in the principal's office at least twice a week," remembers Tess, Kevin's mom. "He was striking other kids, fighting on the playground, even head-butting on occasion. He wasn't afraid to talk back to adults. The principal said he was a very smart kid, but he had a strong spirit and it was going to bring him down." Tess was concerned that Kevin might really hurt someone. She was also worried because his teacher, who was in her first year of teaching, didn't know how to handle Kevin's hyperactive and inattentive behavior in the classroom.

When Kevin entered third grade, Tess decided to homeschool her son to give him the one-on-one attention he seemed to need. Yet, at home, things got worse instead of better. "He challenged me at every turn. He was argumentative and wouldn't do his assignments. I couldn't discipline him," says Tess. It wasn't until a home-school counselor began to review Kevin's history that his behavioral disorders were identified. Kevin is now in treatment for ADHD and ODD, and his mother reports that his behavior is improving. He is getting along better with adults and children and is back in public school.

It can have serious consequences. CD behaviors may include running away from home, skipping school, or lying to parents and teachers. Those with CD may commit illegal acts, such as hurting people or animals, stealing, and vandalism. About 25 percent of boys and 8 percent of girls with ADHD also have CD.

Diving Into Your Gene Pool

Thanks to your parents, you have more than 100,000 genes, which determine things such as the color of your hair, the size of your feet, and how tall you'll be. Scientists have learned that ADHD is a genetic disorder. This means it can be passed down from parent to child through the genes.

Research shows that if an adult has ADHD, there is more than a 50 percent chance that his or her child will inherit it. Studies among identical twins found that when one had ADHD, there was almost an 80 percent chance the other had it as well. Children with ADHD usually have one close relative with the disorder, such as a parent, aunt, or grandparent. It's also common for several brothers and sisters in the same family to be affected by ADHD.

"There are six kids in my family and, including both my parents, 75 percent of us have ADHD," says Erin, who has combined type ADHD. "We aren't very close, to be honest. We don't relate well to one another. We're overly competitive and too sensitive—always getting mad and hurting each other's feelings. It's an emotional roller coaster in my family."

Although scientists are confident that most cases of ADHD are inherited, they are still wondering exactly what is being handed down and how it is being passed along. No one knows. However, most experts agree that the source of ADHD will likely be traced to several genes, rather than to a single one. If the faulty gene(s) can be found, it's likely that scientists will be able to develop a blood test to screen for the disorder someday.

Searching for a Cause

Since Dr. George Still's early studies of ADHD, scientists have been trying to figure out just what triggers the disorder. In the 1930s, American researchers noticed that some people who'd had encephalitis, a viral infection that affects the brain, were exhibiting symptoms of ADHD (a major encephalitis outbreak had occurred in the United States in 1917–1918). These researchers felt that brain damage resulting from infection, head injury, or problems during birth might be responsible for the disorder. Doctors termed it "brain-injured child syndrome." In the 1950s, when scientists realized that kids who had not suffered brain injury were showing symptoms of hyperactivity, the disorder was renamed "minimal brain dysfunction" or "minimal brain damage." However, as technology progressed, it was found that this explanation accounted for only a small number of cases of ADHD.

In the 1970s, a new theory arose claiming that food additives, preservatives, and artificial colorings were to blame for what was then being referred to as "hyperactivity." Dr. Benjamin Feingold popularized a special diet for kids with ADHD that restricted many food additives and chemicals. It was also suggested that eating too much sugar was at the root of the disorder. Parents were encouraged to reduce their children's sugar intake. In 1982, after thoroughly studying these ideas, the NIH concluded that restricting food additives, preservatives, colorings, and refined sugar helped only about 5 percent of those with ADHD (usually the kids with food allergies).

Today, there is disagreement about the role nutrition plays in ADHD. Some people in the nutritional field say that eating such things as sugar and carbohydrates (such as breads, pasta, and potatoes) can worsen ADHD symptoms, while consuming foods that contain omega-3 fatty acids (such as beans, soy, tuna, and salmon) may help reduce symptoms. However, most scientific research indicates that ADHD does not appear to be affected by the types of foods a person eats, unless that person has a food allergy. Studies show a diet that eliminates certain foods may actually be harmful, because children should eat a wide variety of foods to meet all their nutritional needs.

In the 1970s and 1980s, much of the attention surrounding ADHD focused on the environment. Stress at home, divorce, poor parenting, and loud classrooms were reported to trigger ADHD. Scientists now know that while these conditions may sometimes worsen ADHD symptoms, they are not the reason the disorder occurs.

A Dangerous Connection

In rare cases, ADHD has been linked to exposure to poisons, such as lead-based paint and fumes from leaded gasoline. ADHD has also been linked with fetal alcohol syndrome (FAS), a condition that can cause low birth weight, physical defects, and intellectual difficulties. When a pregnant woman takes drugs, smokes, or drinks alcohol, she increases the risk of harming the developing brain of her baby. Heavy alcohol consumption during pregnancy may cause her child to be born with FAS. Scientists note that many children born with FAS show symptoms of ADHD.

ADHD is like a giant jigsaw puzzle. Researchers have many of the pieces, but some are still missing. What exactly causes the disorder? How is it passed from generation to generation? Can ADHD ever be cured? After more than one hundred years of study, scientists are still seeking these answers. New technologies are giving them a window into the human brain, revealing some startling new clues about this mysterious disorder.

Four

Mysteries Within
the Brain

"Having ADHD is like seeing a color differently than everyone else sees it," explains Sarah, a sixth grader. "I always thought everybody saw yellow the same way. I had to realize my yellow wasn't the same as yours. The things that make it hard for me to learn, like people talking quietly in class or somebody mowing the lawn outside, don't necessarily bother anybody else."

ADHD is considered to be a neurobiological disorder. This means it is related to how the brain works. Scientists have discovered that people with ADHD have differences in their brains compared to those who do not have the disorder.

These variations have been found in brain chemistry, function, and makeup.

Your brain is the control center for your entire body. Inside the brain, more than 100 billion nerve cells, called neurons, are constantly relaying messages to each other. This network of nerve cells looks like a miniature freeway system, with roads branching out in all directions. When

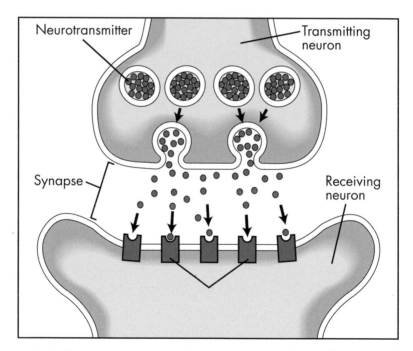

In the brain, messages travel between nerve cells with the help of chemicals called neurotransmitters. In those with ADHD, a deficiency in one or more neurotransmitters may cause the nerve cell not to work properly.

you listen to your teacher, read a book, or do your homework, neurons send out rapid-fire electrical impulses that relay this information throughout the "highways" of your brain and central nervous system. Neurotransmitters, such as dopamine, serotonin, and norepinephrine, help send messages from one neuron to the next.

Scientists conclude that, in those with ADHD, one or more neurotransmitters are working inefficiently. "Some people have more of certain chemicals [in the brain] and some people have less of them. We think that many people who have less develop the symptoms of ADHD," explains Dr. Paul Wender, ADHD expert and distinguished professor of psychiatry, emeritus, at the University of Utah School of Medicine.

Research has shown that certain drugs, such as stimulants like methylphenidate (Ritalin) and amphetamines (Adderall, Dexedrine) and some antidepressants, appear to help regulate the brain's production and functioning of neurotransmitters. A new, nonstimulant drug called atomoxetine (Strattera) has been found to enable more of the neurotransmitter norepinephrine to be available for brain cell communication. In most people with ADHD, these medications help improve self-control, hyperactivity, working memory, handwriting, academics, and other problems associated with the disorder. (For more in-depth information about the medications used to treat ADHD, see Chapter Six: Meeting the Challenge.)

Making the Connection

In 1937, U.S. physician Charles Bradley was trying to find a drug that would help ease spinal tap headaches in children. (A spinal tap involves extracting fluid from the spinal column with a needle. A common aftereffect is a splitting headache.) He discovered, quite by accident, that Benzedrine helped to calm some of his patients with behavioral disorders. Benzedrine is a stimulant, meaning it raises heart rate, blood pressure, and activity level. Bradley was surprised to find that it decreased the symptoms of ADHD. Today, scientists know that stimulants help normalize an underaroused brain and central nervous system, though they aren't exactly sure how the medication does this.

Brain Breakthroughs

Along with discovering variations in the brain chemistry of those with ADHD, scientists have also found differences in the way ADHD affected brain functions. In 1990, Dr. Alan Zametkin of the National Institute of Mental Health in Washington, D.C., used positron emission tomography (PET) to scan the brain activity of adults with ADHD symptoms. PET technology tracks a short-lived radioactive substance

In most people with ADHD, medications help improve self-control, hyperactivity, working memory, handwriting, academics, and other problems associated with the disorder.

as it travels through the arteries of the brain. The dose of radiation received is equal to about two chest x-rays, so it is not considered to be harmful to adults. (Children should not be exposed to any unnecessary radiation, so no children were part of this study.) When compared with the brain functions of a person without ADHD, the PET brain scans revealed that the adults with ADHD symptoms had reduced activity in certain parts of the brain, including the frontal lobe, an area that is responsible for attention and self-control.

Functional magnetic resonance imaging (fMRI) is the newest development in brain-imaging technology. Functional MRI uses strong magnets and radio waves to track blood flow through the brain. It can be used on children with ADHD because it is painless, does not involve radiation, and there are no known risks (no substances are injected into the patient). A person is placed on a moveable bed that slides into a tube surrounded by a large magnet. The fMRI scanner takes computerized pictures of the brain while a person is doing such things as reading, imagining, solving a problem, or even looking at artwork. Increased blood flow to a given area means more activity is going on in that section of the brain. Using fMRI, scientists can map what part of the brain a person is using to perform a particular task.

"Different parts of your brain handle certain types of thinking skills," explains Dr. Fernette Eide, assistant professor of neurology at the University of Washington in Seattle, Washington. "Normally, the back part of your brain is responsible for sensations, such as vision, sound, and spatial perception. The front part of your brain takes care of things like motor skills, attention, decision-making, memory, and sequential processing. What we've found is that there's more activity in the front part of the brain in non-ADHD kids and more activity in the back of the brain in ADHD kids," says Dr. Eide. "This means those with ADHD may be more sensitive to sound and visual stimulation. A noisy classroom, too many things on the walls, or too much on the page can be difficult for them. Yet, because they have heightened auditory and visual sensitivity, they often do very well on computers."

"There's more activity in the front part of the brain in non-ADHD kids and more activity in the back of the brain in ADHD kids," says Dr. Eide.

Mind Matters

In 2002, a ten-year study done by the National Institute of Mental Health found that the brains of kids with ADHD were 3 to 4 percent smaller than the brains of those without the disorder. The differences were observed with magnetic resonance imaging (MRI). MRI uses the same magnetic technology, equipment, and procedure as fMRI, but provides only a structural view of the brain. It does not track blood flow or brain activity. MRI scans thin cross-sections of the body that can be used to create three-dimensional images. The decade-long study looked at the brains of more than 150 kids with ADHD and found that the more severe a person's ADHD symptoms, the smaller certain sections of the brain were. What does this mean? Researchers don't yet know for sure. However, they do say that these findings should not be viewed as bad news, because brain size is in no way connected to intelligence.

Scientists say it is important to note that people with ADHD are not brain damaged, mentally ill, or stupid. Studies show having ADHD has no impact on how smart or talented people are. In fact, some of history's most brilliant and creative minds, including Wolfgang Mozart, Leonardo da Vinci, Pablo Picasso, Henry Ford, Thomas Edison, Ernest Hemingway, Albert Einstein, and General George Patton reportedly showed signs of ADHD.

Some of history's most brilliant and creative minds, including Wolfgang Mozart, Leonardo da Vinci, Pablo Picasso, and Henry Ford, reportedly showed signs of ADHD.

As they continue to study the brain-ADHD connection, scientists are working to better understand the biological basis of ADHD. They still have many unanswered questions, but advancing technology is helping them to fit more pieces of the ADHD puzzle in place. "Now that we have a more sophisticated understanding of the brain systems involved in ADHD, I'm convinced that within my lifetime, we will have the 'golden standard test' for ADHD," says Dr. Judith Owens, director of the Learning Attention and Behavior Program (LAB) at the Child Development Center at Rhode Island Hospital. "Eventually, there will be a genetic screen or a functional MRI test available to confirm the diagnosis. It may not be in the next five or ten years, but it will happen. We're very close."

Five

Pinpointing ADHD

"No matter what I do, it's never enough," says Corey, a ninth grader with hyperactive-impulsive ADHD. "I'm failing math right now. I'm starting to think, 'What's the point?' Sometimes, it's so frustrating I want to quit."

Corey is not alone. In fact, 30 percent of kids with ADHD drop out of school (compared to a 10 percent dropout rate for the general population). Frequently, kids with ADHD find their mental disorder takes a huge toll on their lives. They may not understand why their world is crumbling, only that it appears to be their fault. This can lead to problems with self-esteem, a person's belief in his or her worth and value as a human being.

"My behavior was so bad that, in first grade, I was asked not to be in the class photo," remembers Marco, who has combined type ADHD. "I am always the one everybody looks at when something goes wrong. If there's even a nickel missing in class, I'm blamed for it."

"By the time a child with ADHD reaches middle school, and they aren't achieving or fitting in, they begin to realize 'I'm different,'" explains ADHD expert Dr. Lisa Weyandt, professor of psychology at Central Washington University in Ellensburg, Washington. "Those negative messages that have been coming at them for eleven years are compounded, and their self-esteem takes a big hit. They hear messages like 'you're lazy,' 'you'll never amount to anything,' or 'if you'd just listen and try harder you could do it,' and pretty soon they begin to own it. They may lose confidence in themselves and what they are capable of doing."

Research shows that kids with ADHD who don't get help for their disorder are at higher risk for depression, substance abuse, car accidents, speeding tickets, and engaging in criminal activity. As adults, they are less likely to go to or finish college. They have higher divorce rates, increased problems getting along with coworkers, and are fired from their jobs more frequently than those without the disorder. ADHD researchers emphasize that early identification and treatment is key to helping people with the disorder live happy, well-adjusted lives now and in the future.

ADHD: From the Inside

Step into the shoes of some kids with ADHD to view the world as they do.

"You know what it's like when you go to the mall at Christmastime? There's music playing and it's so crowded you can't think of what store you want to go to. That's what ADHD is like: mass confusion. You hear everything that's going on around you, even the smallest things, like someone tapping his shoe or a bird singing outside. You try to put all the distractions out of your head, but it's hard because there's just so much coming at you."

—*Doug (combined type ADHD)*

"I had no idea what was wrong with me. I just knew that I couldn't do the things that other people did. My life felt like I was walking into a movie at the middle instead of the beginning and I was always trying to cover up so no one would notice that I didn't know what I was doing."

—*Molly (inattentive type ADHD)*

"There are times I simply have to move. If I have a pencil, I'll play with the pencil. It takes a lot of effort to settle down. That's the thing that people don't get. When you have ADHD, you have to keep focusing to stay in control. It's constant work."

— *Nick (hyperactive-impulsive type ADHD)*

Identifying ADHD

Just as it is critical to identify ADHD early, it is equally important, experts say, not to rush too quickly to judgment. Someone who has problems with attention, hyperactivity, and impulsivity may have ADHD, or there may be another problem. To help diagnose ADHD, a health professional such as a pediatrician, psychologist (an expert in human behavior), or neurologist (a doctor who specializes in the study of the brain and central nervous system), will carefully review a child's symptoms. He or she will also collect information from a variety of sources before reaching any conclusions (remember, there is no clear test for ADHD). Parents, counselors, teachers, doctors, family members, and the child being reviewed will all contribute their observations and opinions. The material gathered usually includes the following:

Medical Exam: A physical exam is necessary, because other health issues can sometimes be mistaken for ADHD. Allergies, diabetes, sleep disorders, eating disorders, depression, ear infections, and hearing or vision problems can all affect attention span and behavior. Poor handwriting and motor skills may reflect neurological problems in the brain. Learning disabilities may account for underachievement and difficulties with reading, spelling, writing, and math. Autism, mental retardation, and many developmental disorders may also have symptoms associated with ADHD. A thorough checkup will rule out any health problems that might be producing ADHD-like symptoms.

School Evaluation: Teachers and counselors will be asked to fill out questionnaires that detail their views and experiences with the child. A psychologist, counselor, or teacher will also observe the child at different times and in different locations, such as the lunchroom, a classroom, and the playground. Grades, attendance records, and reports from standardized tests will also be compiled.

Family Interviews: More than 60 percent of kids with ADHD first show symptoms of the disorder during their preschool years. Input from parents and family members about a child's present and past is crucial. Parents will find themselves answering questions on everything from complications during childbirth to the baby's first steps to their child's current table manners. Parents will also fill out questionnaires giving more details about their family's home life, stress levels, and family history of ADHD.

Child Evaluation and Interview: Through questionnaires, tests, observations, and one-on-one interviews, a health professional will talk with the child under review. If that child happens to be you, you will be asked about your life at home and at school. You will be encouraged to share your feelings and experiences as you talk about your relationships with family and friends. You should not feel embarrassed or judged. It is important that a therapist or doctor gather as much information as possible so that an accurate diagnosis can be made. Tests to measure for learning disabilities and achievement may be given. A psychological exam may also be valuable in looking for other medical issues that often accompany ADHD, such as depression, anxiety, oppositional defiant disorder, and conduct disorder.

ADHD: Over-diagnosed or Overblown?

It's estimated that between 3 and 5 percent of all school-age kids in the United States have ADHD. Some health professionals argue that doctors are over-diagnosing the disorder, mistaking things such as learning disabilities, anxiety, and hearing and vision problems for ADHD. They worry that children under the age of five are being misdiagnosed and medicated for a disorder they may not even have. However, the NIH and the American Medical Association have studied the issue and agree that, generally, the disorder is not being over-diagnosed in the United States (in fact, in some areas of the country, the disorder appears to be under-diagnosed). Statistics show that only about half of all U.S. children with ADHD are getting the treatment they need. Scientists say that worried health professionals should also note that ADHD is found in children throughout the world. Other countries, such as Canada, Japan, and Germany, are reporting even higher rates of ADHD than the U.S.

When all of the reports, interviews, questionnaires, and evaluations are complete, they must be carefully weighed. Does the child meet the criteria for having ADHD as defined by the American Psychiatric Association (DSM-IV) (see chart on page 21)? Does the evidence point toward ADHD? A diagnosis of ADHD is subjective, or based on the opinion of the person who is collecting and reviewing the information. Sometimes, it can be helpful to get more than one viewpoint on the matter.

Once ADHD has been diagnosed, what happens? Read on to learn about ways to treat the disorder and to discover how kids with ADHD are living happily and succeeding.

Six

Meeting the
Challenge

" I've always had trouble staying organized, but when I hit middle school last year, with six different classes, I really got overloaded," says Willow, a seventh grader with inattentive ADHD. "I've been working with a counselor, learning how to get organized and improve my study habits. I might have to deal with ADHD for the rest of my life, and I need to know how to handle it."

There is no cure for ADHD, but with help, most people with the disorder can get their lives back on track. Choosing a treatment program for ADHD can be overwhelming. Professionals frequently disagree about which ones work best.

Also, because ADHD symptoms can vary greatly, a method that works for one person may not work well for another.

In 1999, the National Institute of Mental Health and the U.S. Department of Education reported the results of a fourteen-month study of four different plans for treating ADHD. It was the first long-term study ever done on ADHD treatment. Scientists found that a two-pronged approach—medication plus behavioral counseling—proved the most effective way to handle the disorder. "Of course, it's not a 'one-size-fits-all' kind of thing," explains ADHD therapist Dr. Judith Owens. "You have to find the right package for each child." That treatment "package" may include one or more of the following:

- medication
- counseling (behavioral therapy, support group, and/or family therapy)
- educational plan

This chapter will explore how each of the methods mentioned above may be used, separately or combined, to treat ADHD.

Medication: Prescription for Change

About half of all U.S. kids diagnosed with ADHD take stimulant medications as part of their treatment program. Methylphenidate (Ritalin), amphetamines (Dexedrine,

Adderall) and pemoline (Cylert) are the most commonly prescribed stimulant drugs. Antidepressant drugs are sometimes used when stimulants are not effective. In 2002, a new nonstimulant, nonantidepressant drug called atomoxetine (Strattera) was approved for use in treating ADHD.

These medications help regulate neurotransmitters in the brain and enhance communication between nerve cells. Studies show that for most people with ADHD, stimulant medication improves attention, handwriting, working memory, and academic performance, while decreasing symptoms of hyperactivity, aggression, and impulsivity. Side effects may include loss of appetite, weight loss, headaches, stomachaches, moodiness, sleepiness, or insomnia (the inability to fall or stay asleep). Drowsiness may be a sign that too much medication is being taken.

Eleven-year-old Spencer has ADHD, hyperactive-impulsive type, and ODD. His quick temper, refusal to follow rules, blaming others for his actions, and constant battles with adults were causing serious problems at home and at school. His pediatrician advised a combined treatment plan of medication and behavioral modification. However, Spencer's mother, Christine, wasn't so sure that treatment program was a good idea. She had heard some disturbing things in the media about stimulant drugs and was reluctant to give them to her son.

Booming Business

In the past decade, the use of stimulant drugs to treat ADHD and other disorders in this country has skyrocketed from three million prescriptions in 1991 to sixteen million in 2000. The United Nations reports that the United States produces and uses about 85 percent of the world's methylphenidate (Ritalin).

The use of stimulant medication to treat kids with ADHD is a controversial topic in the media. Those who oppose it worry about possible long-term side effects, such as heart and liver damage, addiction, and substance abuse. Yet, most top experts in the field of ADHD point out that stimulants have been around for more than fifty years, and are safe when used properly. Research shows that although about half of kids on stimulants do experience short-term side effects, they are usually minor (appetite loss, insomnia, irritability). Most of these side effects disappear within the first few weeks of taking the medication. So far, long-term use of stimulants has not been shown to cause harm, but scientists are continuing to investigate the issue. Also, there is no indication that using stimulants as directed to treat ADHD leads to addiction or substance abuse. In fact, evidence reveals that those with ADHD are at greater risk for succumbing to alcohol and drug abuse if their disorder is left untreated.

"Millions of children have taken stimulants for ADHD and most of them—not all, but most—have found them to be very helpful," says ADHD expert Dr. Paul Wender. "The medicine isn't going to control you; it's going to help you get better control of yourself and your life. It's not going to make you study; it will help you concentrate so you can study when you want to."

After trying alternative therapies without success, Christine and Spencer decided to opt for stimulant medication. "It has made a big difference in Spencer's behavior," says his mom. "He's cooperative and cheerful, and he gets things done."

About eight out of ten kids with ADHD find that their symptoms improve on one of the stimulant medications. Spencer's pediatrician makes sure he is receiving the proper dosage (usually the lowest dose that proves effective). Spencer also gets regular exercise, plenty of sleep, and makes good nutritional choices—all positive steps that help him manage his ADHD.

Sometimes, kids feel awkward taking medication. They may be embarrassed to take a pill at the school nurse's office or worry about their friends finding out they have a behavioral disorder. "I'm okay with it," says Spencer, who takes his medication once a day, before he goes to school. "All my friends know that I have ADHD, so they know what's going on if I get a little hyper. I don't tell everyone about being on meds, but if someone asks I'll tell them quietly. It's not something to be ashamed of."

Choosing Another Road

About 20 to 30 percent of kids with ADHD do not respond well to stimulants. The medication may not improve their symptoms; in some cases, it may worsen symptoms or cause unacceptable side effects. After stimulants and antidepressants did not appear to be helping eleven-year-old Megan's inattentive ADHD, her parents decided to stop the medication. "She wasn't herself," explains Megan's mom. "All of the sparkle had gone out of her eyes. She lost her appetite, and the medicine gave her headaches. So we started to look around for alternative therapies."

A treatment program that is outside of what is considered to be mainstream medicine is known as an alternative therapy. Some alternative therapies for ADHD include nutritional programs, vitamin supplements, special coordination exercises, and EEG biofeedback (a self-relaxation technique in which a person attempts to alter his or her own brain waves and heart rate while connected to a computer that monitors these vital signs). However, ADHD experts caution that most alternative therapies have not been studied enough to be considered reliable or, in some cases, safe. Many of these unproven methods can also be expensive.

Parents may spend a lot of money on a program only to discover that it doesn't work. Children and Adults with Attention-Deficit/Hyperactivity Disorder (CHADD), a nonprofit organization that promotes ADHD education, says people should be wary of any therapy that:

- does not have clinical trials and control-group studies to back up its claims.
- has not gone through peer review and been published in a scientific journal.
- does not have state licensing and accreditation requirements for practitioners.
- claims to work for everyone and/or claims to cure ADHD.
- does not list contents, side effects, or directions for use.
- is available from only one source.

Megan and her parents decided on a combined approach of behavioral therapy, an educational plan, and a healthier lifestyle of regular exercise and sound nutrition. "It's going better," reports Megan's mother a year and a half into the program. "It's not a perfect solution, but it is working. Most importantly, my daughter is feeling like herself again."

Behavioral Counseling: Setting a New Course

Many kids, such as Megan and Spencer, find that behavioral counseling can help them better manage their ADHD. A licensed therapist, an expert in the field of human behavior, can teach someone with ADHD new ways of responding to certain situations through a technique called behavior modification. Spencer discovered that he had more power over his behavior than he first thought. He learned that a negative reaction on his part usually resulted in a negative outcome, and a positive reaction most often triggered a positive outcome. Spencer realized that when he got angry, he had two choices: he could choose to fuel his anger or try some strategies to put out the flames.

Now, when he gets angry with a friend, instead of hurling words or fists, Spencer takes a different approach. He stops, counts to five very slowly, takes three deep breaths, and thinks about what he really wants to say. If he is still very angry, he might need to take some more time to himself before responding. It isn't always easy to do this, and sometimes Spencer forgets. Even so, it has made a big impact on his relationships with others. Today, he has several close friends, including a best friend—the first he's ever had. In addition, he has learned more effective ways to solve problems and how to set and accomplish goals.

Changing lifelong habits isn't easy. Sometimes, people need a little motivation to help them reach their goals. That's why at home Spencer's parents set up a reward program to encourage appropriate behavior. Once a month, Spencer and his parents select three areas he needs to work on, such as waking up and getting dressed for school on time, bringing home his homework assignments, and finishing all his homework. His mother tacks a chart on the refrigerator to measure his progress one week at a time.

Home Rewards Program			
Name: Spencer, age 11 **Week of:** April 10th – 17th			
	Get up, dressed, & be ready for school on time	Bring home assignments from all classes	Finish Homework	Daily Total
Monday	1	1	0	2
Tuesday	1	1	1	3
Wednesday	1	no homework	no homework	1
Thursday	1	1	0	2
Friday	0	1	1	2
			Weekly Total	10

A home rewards program, where points are earned for completing set tasks, can help many children with ADHD stay organized and focused.

Each time Spencer successfully completes a task, he earns one point. However, if something is left incomplete or is done poorly, Spencer does not receive a point. As Spencer accumulates points, he can "spend" them on one or more prizes from the Rewards Menu, which he helped create.

Home Rewards Menu	
Reward	**Points Needed**
Special snack (make popcorn/cookies)	2
Video games or computer time	3
Remote control airplanes	4
Rent or go to a movie	4
Ask a friend to sleep over	8
Play lasertag	9
New compact disc	15

A rewards menu allows points to be "traded in" for special treats and activities. The menu can be updated often to keep the rewards fresh.

Spencer can choose to spend his points every day for a smaller reward, or "save" his points for a bigger prize. It is his choice. The rewards don't cost a lot and most involve activities he likes to do, such as watching movies or having a friend spend the night. Spencer and his parents change the rewards each month so he gets to do some new and interesting things. Sure, it is fun to get a special privilege when he behaves well, but "the best thing," says Spencer, "is that my mom and dad are proud of me. And I'm proud of myself."

Spencer's parents realized they had to make some changes in their habits too. They began establishing clear rules at home and consequences for Spencer's inappropriate behavior. They discovered the importance of remaining consistent and following through with consequences. This way, Spencer knows what to expect when his behavior isn't appropriate. His mom and dad have also learned more about how ADHD affects behavior and aren't as hard on him as they once were. "We've found that he does much better sitting and listening for long periods of time if he's allowed to fidget with his hands," explains Garrett, Spencer's dad. "I had to realize that Spencer was paying attention as best he could when it looked to me as though he wasn't. A big lesson here is that we all experience the world differently."

As part of his therapy, Spencer joined a local ADHD support group for kids his age. Once every two weeks, he goes to a meeting headed by a social worker to make new friends, talk about his experiences, and encourage other young people with ADHD. He says the support group has helped him realize he is not "weird," and that there are plenty of kids with ADHD who are facing some of the same struggles he is.

Spencer's parents also sought family therapy, a type of group counseling that includes every member of the family.

Getting Along

ADHD can put a great deal of stress on relationships with friends and family. Whether you have the disorder or know someone who does, here are a few things you can do to strengthen your friendships.

If You Have ADHD ...

- Be respectful of your friends. Try not to grab, punch, or bother them.

- Keep a check on your temper. If you do get angry at someone, be sure to say you are sorry.

- Don't get too bossy. Let other kids make decisions, share ideas, or have a turn to play.

- Encourage and listen to your friends. Be kind, courteous, and caring.

- Don't be afraid to ask for help from teachers, counselors, and parents when you need it.

- Be yourself. True friends will understand your disorder and support you.

If Your Friend/Sibling Has ADHD...

- Give positive feedback. Notice when he or she does something good.

- Don't engage in pointless arguments. Ask an adult to help you resolve bigger conflicts, if necessary.

- Be forgiving. Accept a heartfelt apology.

- Listen and be supportive when he or she is feeling frustrated and needs to talk.

- Offer to help him or her get organized, or lend a hand with homework.

- Learn about ADHD. The more you know, the more you'll understand why he or she "zones out" when you're talking or is uncomfortable in a noisy cafeteria.

The impact of ADHD reaches far beyond the person who has it. Brothers and sisters may feel guilty that they don't have ADHD or worry they will get it. They may resent the attention the child with ADHD is receiving. They may believe it is their duty to be the "perfect" student. Parents may feel guilty, angry, hopeless, or frustrated at the level of disruption the disorder is causing within the family. Family counseling can help improve communication and cooperation skills, and can strengthen family relationships.

Educational Plan: Achieving at School

Eighty percent of kids with ADHD struggle with schoolwork and grades, but an educational plan can help those with the disorder improve their academic performance. Teachers, counselors, and parents may want to develop a specific learning program to help a child succeed in school. Even small changes, such as moving a child from the back of the classroom to the front, can increase his or her concentration and performance.

Some of the other things teachers do to help children with ADHD succeed include posting rules, giving clear verbal and written instructions, offering frequent feedback, keeping the noise level in the classroom low, not cluttering the walls with posters, breaking larger assignments into smaller sections, and, whenever possible, allowing for short breaks. Many kids with

ADHD also find that it is helpful to carry calendars with them. Writing down their schedules, homework assignments, and upcoming tests helps them stay organized.

According to federal law, kids suspected of having ADHD must be evaluated at school at no cost to them and may be eligible for special services. These may include accommodations in the classroom, tutoring, special education, counseling, modified assignments and testing, and health services. Public schools across the United States spend more than $3 billion per year on special services for children with ADHD.

A Bright Future

"I keep a journal. I write down my problems, and things I want to change," says Annie, age fourteen, who has inattentive ADHD. "When I go back and read it, even stuff from a few months ago, I realize I've come pretty far. I never thought I could get A's in school, but now I am. I feel like I can accomplish anything if I take small steps and work hard."

ADHD does not have to keep someone from doing well in school, having close friendships, or achieving his or her goals. For the majority of kids with ADHD, their disorder will continue into adulthood. It's estimated that about twelve million U.S. men and women have ADHD. As adults, many with the disorder find their symptoms are not as severe as they were in childhood, while others may have a harder time striking the right balance. But it can be done. Those who find and stick with a treatment program can live a joyful, productive life.

"It's like people with vision problems," says ADHD expert Dr. Lisa Weyandt. "Once they put their glasses on, they're fine. It's similar with ADHD. If kids are treated, and treated successfully, they can go on to earn college degrees or do whatever it is that they desire. Children with ADHD can definitely succeed in life, but they absolutely need the appropriate treatment and supports."

If you have ADHD, don't be afraid to reach out for help. Living with ADHD may not always be easy. By getting proper treatment and focusing on the many positive, wonderful things you have to contribute to the world, you can meet the challenge. You can reach for and capture your dreams.

Glossary

alternative therapy: a treatment approach that is considered to be outside of mainstream medicine

antidepressants: a group of medications that are sometimes used to treat ADHD

attention-deficit/hyperactivity disorder (ADHD): a behavioral disorder characterized by symptoms of inattention, hyperactivity, and impulsivity that appear before the age of seven, continue for at least six months, and cause frequent difficulties in at least two areas of life; scientists have identified three subgroups of ADHD: inattentive type, hyperactive-impulsive type, and combined type

behavioral disorder: an ongoing pattern of abnormal behavior determined by a person's words, actions, and responses to others that severely affects academic progress, social interactions, and daily life

behavioral modification: an approach to treating ADHD that involves someone with the disorder learning new strategies and skills for coping with and responding to situations

conduct disorder (CD): a behavioral disorder that can occur with ADHD and is more severe in nature than ODD; it is characterized by an ongoing pattern of extreme behavior such as running away from home, skipping school, lying, stealing, assault, and vandalism

fetal alcohol syndrome (FAS): a medical disorder characterized by low birth weight, physical defects, and intellectual difficulties; FAS is connected to heavy alcohol consumption by a child's mother during pregnancy and has been linked to ADHD

genetic disorder: a condition that is inherited, or passed down from one generation to the next, through human genes

hyperactivity: the condition of being physically overactive or mentally restless

impulsive: speaking or acting without first considering the consequences

inattention: failure to focus or pay attention

learning disability: a condition that slows development in a particular academic area, such as reading, spelling, or math

neurobiological disorder: a condition or disorder related to brain chemistry or function

neurologist: a medical doctor who specializes in studying the human brain and central nervous system

neurons: nerve cells that relay messages throughout the brain and central nervous system

neurotransmitters: chemicals found naturally in the brain and central nervous system that aid in the communication between nerve cells

oppositional defiant disorder (ODD): a behavioral disorder that may occur with ADHD and is characterized by an ongoing pattern of disobedient, negative, and hostile behavior toward adults for at least six months

self-esteem: a person's own belief in his or her value and worth as a human being

stimulant medication(s): a particular group of drugs, such as methylphenidate (Ritalin) and amphetamines (Adderall, Dexedrine), that are used in treating ADHD

therapist: a licensed health professional, such as a counselor, psychiatrist, social worker, or psychologist, who has special training to treat mental and behavioral disorders

therapy: an approach to treating a disorder or disease

Further Resources

Books

Beal, Eileen. *Everything You Need to Know About ADD/ADHD.* New York: Rosen Publishing Group, 1998.

Morrison, Jaydene. *Coping with ADD/ADHD.* New York: Rosen Publishing Group, 2000.

Nadeau, Kathleen G. and Ellen B. Dixon. *Learning to Slow Down and Pay Attention: A Book for Kids about ADD.* Washington, DC: Magination Press, 1997.

Williams, Julie. *Attention-Deficit/Hyperactivity Disorder.* Berkeley Heights, NJ: Enslow Publishers, 2001.

Videos

It's Just Attention Disorder: A Video Guide for Kids, C.C. & Company, 1991.

The ABC's of ADD, JKL Communications, 1993.

Online Sites and Organizations

Attention Deficit Disorder Association (ADDA)

1788 Second Street, Suite 200

Highland Park, IL 60035

add.org

ADDA is dedicated to helping those with ADHD lead happier, more successful lives through education, research, and public advocacy. Their Web site covers a variety of ADHD topics, from common misconceptions about ADHD to the latest news on medication. Check out the kid and teen areas for great tips on improving schoolwork and getting along with friends and family.

Children and Adults With Attention-Deficit/Hyperactivity Disorder (CHADD)

8181 Professional Place, Suite 150

Landover, MD 20785

800-233-4050

www.chadd.org

CHADD is a nonprofit organization that supports individuals and families dealing with ADHD while working to educate the public about this challenging disorder. On its Web site, you can learn more about educational rights of children with ADHD, or "Ask the Expert" a question online. You can also find a CHADD chapter and support group near you.

LD Online
The Learning Project
WETA TV, PBS
2775 South Quincy Street
Arlington, VA 22206
www.ldonline.org
This Web site is devoted to educating the public about learning disorders, behavioral disorders, and other health issues. Click on the "Kidzone" for tips on getting organized, good books to read, and links to other ADHD resources.

National Center for Learning Disabilities (NCLD)
381 Park Avenue South, Suite 1401
New York, NY 10016
888-575-7373
www.ncld.org
NCLD is a nonprofit organization that supports children and adults with learning disabilities and promotes public aware-ness. Learn more about the causes and symptoms of various learning disorders, discover ways you can succeed at school, and get plugged into local and national resources.

Index

About the Author

Trudi Strain Trueit is an award-winning health and medical broadcast journalist. As a news reporter for KREM TV (CBS) in Spokane, Washington, her weekly on-air segment, *Your Health*, earned recognition from the Society of Professional Journalists. *Unborn Ethics*, a documentary examining the controversy over genetic engineering, received top national honors from United Press International.

Ms. Trueit's other titles in the Life Balance series include *Eating Disorders* and *Dreams and Sleep*. Also a television weather forecaster, she has written more than fifteen books for Scholastic Press on weather, nature, and wildlife. Ms. Trueit has a B.A. in broadcast journalism and makes her home in Everett, Washington, with her husband, Bill.

Acknowledgements

Special thanks to consultant Dr. Lisa Weyandt, professor of psychology at Central Washington University in Ellensburg, Washington, for her insight and guidance. Also, many thanks to Dr. Judith Owens at the Learning Attention and Behavior Program (LAB) at The Child Development Center at Rhode Island Hospital.